AGAINST DISTANCE

Poems by Peter Makuck

BOA
EDITIONS
LIMITED

AGAINST DISTANCE

Poems by

PETER MAKUCK

BOA Editions, Ltd. ✂ Rochester, NY ✂ 1997

LC #: 96-80094
ISBN: 1-880238-44-6 cloth
ISBN 1-880238-45-4 paper

First Edition
97 98 99 00   7 6 5 4 3 2 1

Publications by BOA Editions, Ltd.—
a not-for-profit corporation under section 501 (c) (3)
of the United States Internal Revenue Code—
are made possible with the assistance of grants from
the Literature Program of the New York State Council on the Arts,
the Literature Program of the National Endowment for the Arts,
the Lannan Foundation, the Sonia Raiziss Giop Charitable Foundation,
the Eric Mathieu King Fund of The Academy of American Poets,
as well as from the Rochester Area Foundation Community Arts Fund
administered by the Arts & Cultural Council for Greater Rochester,
the County of Monroe, NY,
and from many individual supporters.

Cover Design: Geri McCormick
Cover Photo: Ray Scharf
Author Photo: Ric Carter
Typesetting: Richard Foerster
Printed in Canada by Best Book Manufacturers
BOA Logo: Mirko

BOA Editions, Ltd.
A. Poulin, Jr., President
(1938–1996)
260 East Avenue
Rochester, NY 14604

For Leslie Norris

. . . monads haunted by communion
—Henry G. Bugbee

CONTENTS

Part I

Tangier Island — 13
Dogwood Again — 16
After the Perfect Place — 17
Gray Removals — 19
Near the Agua Fria — 21
Catsail — 24
Ocean Fog — 25
After — 27
Close — 29
Chalet in Air — 30
Beyond French Doors — 32
Owl and Heron — 34
Lobsters — 35
Woodsmoke — 37
Against Distance — 39
Hunter — 44
Big Eddy, Upstream of the Grimesland Bridge — 45
Dry Creek — 46
Ritual on Indian Pier — 49

Part II

Leaning Against the Bar at Wrong Way Corrigan's
in Greenville, North Carolina — 53
Not Wasted — 54
Dust Devil — 56
Subchaser — 58
On the Blue Again — 60
Papa — 61
Another Country — 64
Fluteman — 66
Valentine — 69
Bradfords — 71
Sequoia Sempervirens — 73
Above Spanish Forks — 75

Distance at the Dockside Inn — 77
Seascape — 78
Egret — 79
Flying Fish — 82
Day of the Warbler — 84
A Guide to Arrival — 86
Trafficking with Voices — 88

Acknowledgments — 91
About the Author — 93

Part I

TANGIER ISLAND

In memoriam George Marcil, O.F.M.

A mile above the Eastern Shore,
before we turn over water
in a friend's small plane, I see,
on the way to this speck in the Chesapeake,
the interlocking shapes
of green and plowed-brown fields
that put me in mind of Cézannes
I saw first in your class
at St. Francis on the coast of Maine.

Some wrote you off as "Silly George"
because you liked to laugh
with your whole big face,
but this is how you coaxed us
from ourselves to the enlargements
of philosophy and art—
the first for learning how to die, you said
(laughing, of course),
the second for learning how to see.

Climbing from the plane, I see
Maine for a moment—stacks of lobster traps
instead of crab shacks, pots and buoys.
Camera in hand, I'm wandering
these narrow lanes
more with you than my wife and friends.
You're explaining perspective again—

triangles and frames within frames,
light, color, and distance
around that waterman scraping his skiff.
Or how to focus family
headstones in a tiny front yard

where a woman rakes leaves
into a burning pile, the smoke
rising, then flattening in the heavy air
to hover like a huge pair of wings.

At the far end of the island, we turn
and face the distant houses
huddled together, barely above water.
One white steeple
tops the invisible triangle, fixes
the churning clouds and wind-bent trees
in this old Dutch seascape.

On my Renoir report
about "The Boatmen's Lunch,"
you wrote that "*joie de vivre*
is a gift,
and not a basis to evaluate painting."
I didn't know what you meant
until years later
when I saw you for the last time,
chemo-bald but undiminished,
smiling with your whole face,
radiant, like a bulb
before its filaments blow.

This island lives by the crab,
those red commercial emblems
a reminder of what you fought against,
what finally killed all color,
so I aim and focus
the water-doubled reeds of spartina,
still brown
but for a promise of green
at the base of each blade.
The shutter clicks
and a slide of Albrecht Dürer's
wild grasses are alive on our classroom wall.

As we bank toward home, I see
Tangier from the south at 5000 feet
looking like a medieval angel,
tilted forward, ready
to blaze through
a black wall of weather to the west.

DOGWOOD AGAIN

Home from college, I'd leave my reading,
climb the hill through trees behind the house,
listen to a rough wind suffer through
new leaves and, too aware of myself, ask why?

The answer could have been *stone wall*,
wind or some other words. In April, our house
lived in the light of those first white petals
and now I think more about hows than whys—

how, whenever we fished at Pond Meadow,
my father dug a small one up, carefully
wrapped the rootball in burlap, and trucked it
home until our yard blazed white all around,

and how, at Easter, those nighttime blossoms
seemed like hundreds of fluttering white wings.
Again that tree goes into the dark loaded
with envy, those leaves full of light not fading.

And this morning, a fogbright air presses
against the blank white pane and would have us
see the way mist burns from within, shimmers,
slowly parts, and flares upon an even whiter tree,

tinged now with orange, and how a soft fire
runs to the farthest cluster of cross-like petals,
each haloed with clear air, finely revealed.

AFTER THE PERFECT PLACE

Whenever I dawdle up the high rise
of the Carteret Bridge,
drivers behind me hit their horns
because I slow down,
way down,
for that wide spread of marshgrass to the west,
the main and side channels, so many
eelgrass islands and sunfired loops of water
with here and there a lone
egret standing on its shadow.
I want the whole sight to myself,
the stillness of one of those wading birds,
or that single boat
        off in a seaward meander.

So I know that someone
in a harried car up there
wishes he was down here, anchored
in this side channel, lazing
under a cool blue Bimini top.
But cicadas eat up the silence,
the bridge rumbles its concrete slabs
        like distant thunder,
the air itself half sweat,
and not one single bite in an hour.
Now rock from a boombox—
two kids in a brand new Robalo
have dropped anchor across the channel.
It's golden skin,
birthday suits off the stern,
splashtime with Adam and Eve,
jiggle and moon up the ladder,
giggle and kiss, kiss and laugh,
and I'm not even here
when they disappear below the gunnels

in that awful need
to be always someplace else.

GRAY REMOVALS

After a night of March winds,
I expect the yard to be blown away,
but my neighbor's out there grinning,
another squirrel in his boxtrap.
Twiggy nests that web the forks of limbs
have withheld the night. And squirrels,
either oblivious, or deliberately mocking,
chase each other, madly spiral his oaks (and mine),
leaping limb to limb, then over the roof,
along the powerline, and into another yard.

My neighbor is determined,
ready to transport his catch
deep into the oblivion of distant woods.
We're overrun, he says. The signs are everywhere.
Rain spilling from the upper gutter—
Squirrels do that. They'll ransack your attic,
beat you out of your hard-earned pecans,
raid the seed in your feeder. Rats,
really just rats he's taking to meet
their country cousins. Same damned family.

      As a kid, I used to shoot them
and nail their pelts to the barn door.
My trigger finger hasn't itched in ages,
but with my neighbor's right reason, I tend to agree,
yet early in the morning, when my body is heavy
and flexes like half-frozen meat,
I'd have them left alone, these gray ghosts,
let them land on my roof with a slap
and wake me with a rain-like patter in the eaves.

Three feet from my desk,
on the raingutter,
like a jeweler with a gem to cut,

it rotates an acorn—crack, then feast.
Its eyes hold mine as it chews.
The air clears, as if someone had focused a lens,
removed a moment from the day
and made it lively forever.
Every time, I'll look up from my work,
take the bait, and be transported,
always confused when released, ready to run.

NEAR THE AGUA FRIA

Off Arizona 17,
walk the arroyo
for a time, then leave it
for a saddle between two peaks. . . .

Turning from the car
that took him to clients
in distant towns, he grinned
at his impulse to stop
for the desert heat,
seeing lupine and larkspur,
cholla and ocotillo in flower
for the first time in years.
Brittlebush too. The air was sweet
as remembering the way
your life can happen
one cactus wren at a time,
that shy singing
into what will soon be dark.

From a trance of fragrance,
he snapped awake at the rattle
of feathers, quail,
a quick black track
in silver light above sage,
studied the drop
between rocky outcrop, clouds
of palo verde below,
and five saguaro
staggered like sentinels
across the short valley floor.

Where the trail bottomed
before climbing again, he stopped
for water, hearing her voice:

Always take water,
mark your trail,
and tell someone
where you are going. . . .

Or where you have been, he thought,
watching a clutch of ocotillo
barely stir its eight-foot candles
tipped with scarlet flames.
Birds sang to each other,
unseen as the air, then ceased.

At the summit,
a vast view held him
until he saw her
off the trail at a tripod easel, serene,
her hair gold as the lowering sun.
Though the sound behind her
could have been a cougar,
she never turned her attention
from the one-armed saguaro
clustered with crimson
as it was down slope, spiny on top,
but with a kestrel on canvas
that wasn't there.

Sweaty and winded,
taken by this total attention,
he went for the water again
and gave the scene time
to arrange itself—
the scarlet tips of ocotillo,
wren song, red brome, and eddies of scent,
each detail
down to her blue-handled brushes.
Then easing away,
listening to the voice,
he repeated,

walk the arroyo
near the Agua Fria
then leave it
for a saddle between two peaks,

marking the track
that months from now
would lead him back
to a past quenching
as cold water.

CATSAIL

Out on the edge
between ocean and a sky
that swallows light,
     red, yellow, and green,
bright as a foreign flag,
it catches the wind
and something inside
about color,
the secret of difference,
how it changes
what we are,
makes us feel
we could walk out
on that watery sunpath
into another country
where, like children,
we would do little but
play with the quiet
and learn our colors again.

OCEAN FOG

This could still be sleep,
the way dream
untunes the familiar,
dawn hanging curtains
that part then close
upon a glimpse of boats
around a red buoy
that groans
at dangerous moves
before the gun
in some unlikely regatta.

This drifting white
does tricks with sound,
muffles an emptiness
that could have a tanker
in no time
bearing down on a small boat,
but the air enchants,
drenched with light that glows
like pure wool waiting
to ignite into nothing,
but not yet, not yet,

and boats become
trawl doors dangling
or tuna towers
detached and floating,
then disappear,
surviving only as sound,
the deep gargle of diesels
until they emerge
developed slowly whole
around the red groaner
as if trying to awake

to some new version
of themselves
before fading again.

Then the sun, in patches,
burns a scene into view,
and each antenna,
cabin, mast, and boom attaches
at last to its proper hull
and each boat,
in circus procession,
moves seaward from the bridge—

not a lyrical schooner,
but a trawler bleeding
rust from its scuppers,
a tall black and red tug,
a homemade houseboat,
Tom and Huck in a skiff,
two flashy Makos with T-tops,
and then—
fancy's final touch
where first shall be last—

a huge Hatteras, him and her
on the fly bridge
swaying like Brit royalty
on the back of an elephant,
and *Just Foolin*
in fool's gold on the stern,
the fog at last finished
with this private Fellini.

AFTER

In the low afternoon light,
a row of cottonwoods led us out of Santa Cruz,
a small cemetery off in the desert.

That day, a few days before Christmas,
your father in front with me, I kept seeing your mom
not there in the back beside you

and him, as I drove, stare through
the passing mesquite to some other place perhaps,
silence enforcing a distance.

Lame, he had held my arm,
looked down at the unhealed turf, then crossed himself,
thin shoulders quaking. I looked

beyond the wall, across
the creosote flats, and watched a coyote drag something
limp toward a culvert.

Back in the car, I kept seeing,
tethered to stones, all those mylar balloons—"Feliz Navidad"
or "Te quiero" in the shape of a heart—

emblems of another culture,
telling us how far from home we were, the balloons
tormented in the desert wind.

Before houses again rose up
and the lights of Phoenix hid a perfect indigo sky
where stars began to glimmer,

we stopped at a crossroads light,
emptiness everywhere but this rancho of cracked adobe,
chickens and a single goat.

In front of the corral,
a Mexican sat on a kitchen chair, his face tipped back
and bronzed like a mask.

We watched a young woman
trim his hair, then lean down for a whisper and a kiss,
their faces wrinkled with laughter,

making me ease the car ahead
to center and frame them in the open gate at our side,
while we waited for the light.

Your father turned
and watched them too, and though his face was shadowed,
I saw his features tighten and focus.

After the woman ran her fingers
through her husband's long dark hair and trimmed again,
your father closed his eyes and smiled.

Their voices came inside
but they never looked our way as we watched, oblivious
as a family photo

finished by a boy in a red bandana
entering from the right, chasing a black chicken
and making it fly.

Before we left that crossroads
with whatever it was we needed, the light went green
two or three times, I think.

CLOSE

This house has lots of breathing space,
bathrooms to spare—
no need to look for the line of light
under that one door
that would keep me from barging in.
No bumping in the narrows
of the midnight hall, my father
sleepwalking past.
Yet some sound or mood of light
still puts me in that tiny house.
I can hear their nightly closeness.
I can listen to their dream
plans coming through thin walls
into the held breath of the hallway dark
before college made our house
look small and poor.
Those holidays home,
it is always late, too late in the kitchen.
Surprised, my mother lowers
her glass from view.
A moon fills the window behind her,
a red face looking in. My father
snores, just down the hall
in the bed that used to be mine.
Soon he will sleepwalk again,
moving farther away, drifting
into a breathless world beyond the stars.
In fact, he already has.
My mother and I sigh at the same time.
I watch her shuffle into the dim hall
toward a realm unreachably distant,
but still as close as air.

CHALET IN AIR

In that early winter light,
plunking down a plate of bacon
and eggs she said
would stick to my ribs,
my mother did her irksome slang song,
hovering near,
telling me I ate like a bird,
urging me: "Eat up, eat up.
Stoke that furnace."

Then, still warbling
at the window above the sink,
she watched
the small chalet I'm watching now,
made by my father,
authentic right down to the roof shakes,

suspended from a limb,
ten feet above dead grass,
its dormers and decks spilling seed
with each new arrival,
bucking on its fishline,
busier at breakfast than McDonald's:

sparrows, titmice, and chickadees,
but no fancy riffs
from a mockingbird's tunebag,
not this time of year—
just demotic song
that gets through glass,
swirls down the porches of our ears.

A cardinal, a wide female,
with dun feathers and orange beak,
offers the only color

until a gust of waxwings hits the oak,
their pearl gray bodies tinged with pink,
tailbars yellow as the juice in my glass,
but come from a distance
farther than Florida
to stoke my furnace,
to give me something
that sticks to my ribs.

BEYOND FRENCH DOORS

We took a chainsaw to the room's one window,
widened the frame, lengthened it ceiling to floor,
braced the lintel with steel,
each change leading to another—a porch,
a roof, sidelights, a brick walk, and so on.

But now more light
reveals a rivering grain in the floor planks
and moving through this remodeled room,
I find myself stalled again and again
willing to forget old scores,
family and friends.

Beyond the doors,
fur up and taut for attack,
the black manx and calico square off over turf,
a forgotten cardinal above them turning
brighter with each turn
        of the hanging feeder
middle distance in this new depth-of-field.

With each moment, I forget even more.
How can one match such lucid stillness?
I'm all eyes
for the endless patience of pine boughs,
blowing like a girl's full sleeves,
        adjusting themselves to the wind,
old insults and betrayals
        light as those dead leaves
in a brief churning that crosses the yard.

A rosy finch flashes to the hedge.
At the threshold, near my feet, a wobble
      of dappled light disappears.
I open the doors, step out, and clap my hands.
The manx and calico scatter in the cold sweet air.

OWL AND HERON

After an all-day drive through August air,
I walk out on the wooden planks of a bridge.
Not a breeze thinks of stirring,
the day going down in flames
behind some Carolina rib shack by a river.
Suddenly, a silver canoe quickens the scene.
The current is black and fast
but he's all ease against it
this old man, all ease and skill,
and just before he's taken by the bend,
the blade of his paddle flashes
and I could swear I see
a tall white bird take flight, flap
behind its long neck, glide, and hide itself
in tall slackwater reeds.
A breeze starts in the tree tops,
a descending whisper, a long cool touch.

Last January, on my way to friends
with jars of apple-jack
for a cold cabin afternoon, I saw
a white-bibbed owl; it swooped
across the dirt road, this bird
I had only seen in my father's shed—
a picture on a cigar box lid.
From a high dead limb, it dove
and flapped toward the fastness of deeper woods,
that great owl on the wing
deeper and deeper with its hunting light.

Owl and heron light the air
of the long hard dark between.

LOBSTERS

The seaward channel bends by a salvage yard
of hulks, a ruined ferry, its stacks rusting in shallows,
a tug, tipped on its side, bleeding from hull plates.

At the end of a meander, a white egret,
a reflection stilted and poised above the mud flats, poised
even with a junkyard dog barking along the bank.

Larry, friend since the fifth grade nuns,
hits the throttle, steers his workboat into the same searoad
attack-subs from Groton have taken for years,

the town and the gold-cross steeple standing
behind the cove on a hill, slipping astern but never gone.
The sun burns down. No air in the river

until finally, off Ledge Light, a breeze comes down,
like a laying on of hands, and cools my brow,
a kind of balm for last night's beer and smoke and noise.

I hook the first blue buoy and haul the warp,
heavier than memory, until the trap breaks water,
a nightmare tangle of kelp, claws, feelers, and eyes on stalks.

We measure each carapace and toss back
the shorts, only small talk between us, not like last night
and our wrangle about the Haves and the Have-nots,

rich bastards grabbing theirs, him telling me
that too many books have put me in a fool's paradise,
made me forget my own. My father, it's true, had

battered hands, but he scattered crumbs to the backyard birds
and loved to read—the sky, those clouds
that build, bulge, then thin, like a dramatic story that heals.

And I didn't know "diddly" about the "real" world.
Who does? Westward a sailboat tilts on glitter, to the east,
a wall of black warns us we're in for a soaking.

Try to work faster. Band each claw to keep them
from duelling, devouring each other. Rebait with bunkies,
stuff the net full of stink, thumb the latches,

shove each trap from the gunnel
to settle like a depth charge into the dark real world of Haves
and Have-nots, then dance free of the outcoiling rope.

Once, with no regrets, I turned in a headboat
for tossing trash. But now those clouds on the build need help
to heighten their blue tucks and folds, bronze their crowns,

let rain slant from their black bellies
and touch us with some kind of help. I hook the buoy
and haul, imagining nothing has changed,

thinking of the egret back on the flats making light
of that ruined fleet. The last trap breaks water to an applause
of slapping tails. Larry counts the bodies and laughs

at the line squall that leaves us soaked, and him singing
"Still crazy after all these years."
The air grows orange in the east. It's late summer.

Ocean Beach from five hundred yards offshore
seems much smaller than when the steepled town behind it
had no bounds and told me daily it was mine.

WOODSMOKE

Sometimes the sight of it
curling blue
from brick chimney
on a rusty tin roof

or the scent of it
drifting on a cold day
puts an edge on things,
reminds me

we were almost poor
forked creatures
those frosty mornings,
our country home no

fairytale cottage,
sharp whispered phrases
I shouldn't have heard,
and never mind

what mortgage means,
Mr. Nosey Nicholas,
my mother said,
my father in a sweat

after long sessions
of sledge and maul
until the new furnace,
(our first step up)

finally took my job
of feeding the stove—
twigs to fiery licks,
the heavy breathing

of the flue,
and my father too
stacking his splits,
their bright insides

lighting the dark
those frozen mornings
before he left for the first
of his three daily jobs,

the cold never again
so warm.

AGAINST DISTANCE

It was toward the end of the pier,
toward the shark rigs,
toward guys cracking beers and jokes
where fathers and kids used to fish all day,

I heard, then saw
        some forty yards off
a boy in a black tube caught fast in a rip tide,
waving an arm that couldn't be seen
by anyone, it seemed, but me.

In a few seconds, I knew,
he'd quit the tube and try for shore,
so I dove,
unable even later to remember
dropping my rod and reel,
removing sandals or climbing the rail,
seeing only the reflected arrow
of a body break the surface,
my lucky face
escaping a web of lines and hooks.

I swam toward something remembered,
the long shadow of Jack the Greek,
my uncle's buddy, breaking through
a quicksilver membrane,
his face pinched,
the arm reaching down, down,
to pluck me back into air.

I reached the boy
with just enough breath to blurt,
    "Stay with the tube,"
then over and over told him not to worry,
though I did

because the current was wicked and fast
and the pier hurried back and away.

Figures at the rail grew small,
and none I could see were running for help.

The valve stem bubbled hard
and boats I had seen from the pier
now disappeared.

Though he didn't cry,
his chin wrinkled like the stone of a peach,
his eyes grew huge,
        hazel and round,
a small worm scar on his cheek
scarlet from the sun,
my pep talk
doing little to soften all the taut
white lines of his face.

The clouds, mockingly,
swam at an easy pace toward the beach.

Never had I been so distant from shore
except in a boat,
and thought about the reef sharks
you often see around the end of the pier.
        "Don't splash," I said.

Besides, kicking was useless.
The rip would leave us far out when it quit.
The coast, at the top of swells, showed itself
        a long white line of sand,
a lime colored band of live oak and yaupon,
        and the beautiful faces of homes.

E.T. was his favorite film,
        baseball his favorite game.

His father lived in another town.
"Mom's under the pier with her friend."

Less than an hour ago
I had stood on the porch of our rental,
the sky all flickered white and torn with gull cries
over an ocean going from gloss to rough
where krill massed and mackerel sickled through
on a changing tide toward the pier.
I tapped the window, waved my arms,
pointed to the action,
did a dumb show of reeling like mad
but the kids,
enthralled by a video game,
were shadowy figures
drowning in an air-conditioned room,
glassed against the water and sand
with cartoon bombs detonating louder than the surf—
no interest in the older game
of cast and wait,
mackerel flanks all silver flecked with bronze.
So off I went with one of the five rods
I had just rigged
toward the long, tall pier in the distance.

No one was coming.
Moments got longer.
Water slapped at the tube.
The valve stem bubbled away.
And something sinister began.
A faraway house
alone on an undeveloped dune
        became a face
with wide apart dormers for eyes,
a porch-roof nose in between,
twin brick chimneys for ears.
The face, like some false god,
commanded belief, gloated,

then fixed us
with a sunstruck paneglass eye.
For a moment,
just a moment, I was ready to believe,
to sacrifice whatever it wanted,
until we drifted up to a raft
of gulls that rose and broke apart
like some selfish memory
I wanted to forget—
          an eighth-grade nun
who knew I'd come to no good end
for laughing always at the wrong time

as I did just then, a panicky cackle
that frightened the boy
who let go a cry, lonely and lost
as any I had ever heard, as if his mind
or mine had snapped,
then grew calm as the current.

At some point, unnoticed, the wind
turned about
and came at our backs with a push,
and kicking together, but so as not to splash,
we cheered ourselves, as the beach,
in glimpses at the top of swells,
          came slowly,
slowly closer, and that face
became a house again,

knots of tiny bathers below it,
and lone, dark figures bending for shells.

We kicked and rested.
Shouts and cries came over the surf
far from the pier
          where our toes touched sand again.
Children ran and dove, shellers stooped,

but no one arrived to wrap us
in blankets or hugs.
Unnoticed, we had been swept away.
The boy, shaking water, left his tube,
splashed from the shallows,
and ran toward the pier
where his mother
and the man who might one day be a father
returned to retrieve that leaky black tube
and look about
for another man now hidden
above them on the fishing pier.

  In the afterlife
of the cottage front room,
I lay on the sofa,
trying to focus that other world
within this one
wavering its magic light on the ceiling,
heavenly proof
of the buoyancy still in my limbs,
angels laughing around me
at sitcoms and game shows,
me drifting again,
air-conditioned as anyone,
thinking of saving
and of being saved

by a boy
who could have been my son
and kept me from drowning.

HUNTER

Like the heat in this kitchen,
your family at Christmas gets close,
smoke from ashtrays,
kids at Monopoly crying. Adults at dessert
take political aim, one uncle
sulking at his slow spoon, an aunt helping
her outrage with cognac.
The brother-in-law slaps
a kill-shot at a senator's greed,
lights up, and grins.
You wait for the right moment and ease off
to a cool corner
and the wrap-up news:

In the Superstitions,
a hunter is lost. A chopper has found
his truck by Apache Junction,
wife in tears, the mercury taking a dive.
The reporter says he will experience extremes,
and turns out the lights.
Now we see what the hunter sees—a black
cold nothing he will try to outwit
with one pure thought.
The search will continue.
Admit it—you half wish
it was you.

BIG EDDY, UPSTREAM
OF THE GRIMESLAND BRIDGE

By the old plantation
       caving in on its dark histories,
you kill the outboard.

Fall comes to the river
       reluctantly, as if to another stint
on the second shift at Dupont.

Silence reports, No wind.
       One squirrel barks to another—
ambition of the best kind.

Along the surface
       mullet leap and flash, trying to free
themselves of tiny worms that itch.

The boat revolves
       in the enlightened air, each turn
bringing news, almost one's own.

Two crows leave from a high limb.
       An apple thuds in the overgrown orchard.
Its cidery scent fans out.

In the audible light
       bees drill for sweetness, working
only as hard as they have to.

❧

DRY CREEK

We made more noise than beagles
hunting a trailhead that couldn't be found,
then stumbled instead
      the uneven stones
and rocks of an arroyo
down among the cottonwoods.
Two families. Five kids.

Irked by the plan
or stung by some remark,
      I lag behind and listen to them rattle
down the dry wash loud as a flash flood.
December, red-rock desert near Sedona.
      Overcast and cold,
and too late in the day to be hiking.

I stared at the stones
that were loaves, platters, and ovals
—each a different color of quiet—
      until a bird
flashing yellow lifted my eyes
before hiding itself in saltbush
above steep shoulders of the creek.
Sharp outlines of buttes and towers,
cliffs and sandstone ramparts rose around me,
each shape a suggestion: cathedral,
chimney, sleeping chief.

I followed the bird
further across flats clotted with greasewood,
wanting a better look
at what flew up
from that bed of colored stones.
Each step took me closer to boyhood
to my father whispering

that Apaches make no noise,
choosing the right place for each silent foot.

I stopped to listen,
          about to give up
on what I later learned was a grosbeak
when I saw, through a hole
in a scrim of palo verde,
at just the right angle,
the twitching ears of a deer.
I circled behind, saw,
each time I stopped,
through a different break
in the branches, a flank
the color of new-baked bread
inflating with breath,
making one warm place
in the vast cold blue. Several times

she disappeared,
patience bringing her back,
tear-shaped ears, dainty black hooves.
Then she was whole, prone, lying on her side,
head raised and turned
to catch me slow-motion stepping
from a crosshatch of branches
and twigs. I barely breathed,

and when, after a moment,
she lowered her head, that wet black nose,
a white scut, I inched ahead,
close enough to kill
or see myself reflected, tiny,
in the two dark worlds of her eyes,
in this circle of brush, faintly radiant,
my breathing now matched to hers.
Behind me, I heard
or thought I heard, a snicker of wings

and when I turned back,
she was gone.

My breath hung white before my face.
How I could have gotten that close,
such a lack of fear
growing from silence?
I found my way back
to the ringing stones of the creek,

my niece coming out
of shadows, giving me an oval
of smooth white stone that glowed
like her face in the deepening dark.

RITUAL ON INDIAN PIER

The pier was empty,
full of wooden groans,
the seas high,
the onshore drizzle
blowing horizontally.
I met a guy out here
thin and old,
hollow in the temples,
a hook scar on his chin,
his ghostly face smiling
under a shaky lamp.

All night we fished,
outlasted everyone
through a long lull
that broke before dawn
with a school of blues.
Talk didn't matter
but when it came
his accent was shack poor
and hard to read.
That morning
at the cleaning table,
he noticed my hands
had never learned
to use a knife.

So he taught by gesture,
as if ashamed to speak,
spat on the white whetstone
and made small circles with the blade,
angling the steel,
honing an edge without feathers.
His black hand
would stop mine, guide it

in behind the gills to find the bone.
Toothless, he'd laugh,
then I'd watch his hand,
as if by magic,
in one motion, flip the fillet
and peel off the skin.
"Sharp knife do it all," he grinned,
holding the skeletal comb
to the x-ray light,
our ritual finished by gulls.

Tonight,
on the stone he made me keep
in exchange for a few beers, I find
the right angle,
make those same small circles.
His whole face smiled.
"Don't you worry," he said,
"time ain't nothin',"
and guided me through
every last blue,
laughing, covering his mouth,
then pursing his lips
as if kissing himself
or somebody else good-bye.
Years ago.
He must be dead by now.

As I cut these blues,
find the bone and work the knife,
his white whetstone
stands on the rail
against the dark,
like a marker finally set.

Part II

LEANING AGAINST THE BAR AT WRONG-WAY CORRIGAN'S IN GREENVILLE, NORTH CAROLINA

after James Wright

Over my head, I see the green toucan,
taunted into squawking, "Go for it!"
by a red-faced juicer with jesus hair and a pool cue.
Down two smoky stairs by the jukebox
pool balls follow one another
from the table's green field into long dark tunnels.
To my right,
on her bare shoulder, behind a scrim
of long bleached hair, a tattooed butterfly,
the color of crankcase oil, sleeps on and on.
I lean back, as the late news comes on overhead.
A drunk staggers out the door, blind for home.
I have wasted my cash.

NOT WASTED

The stale last odors
of last night's drinkers
bent into fits of laughter
and spilling beer
are no joke,
and cigarette stench
has my gorge on the rise,
the scent of Pine-sol
doing little against
potions that had me
so contagiously funny
and now have me here
dying at our glass doors,
looking to the paradise
of our own back yard
for some kind of help,
a heap of ice from the cooler
still frozen,
glinting where I tossed it
in the new winter rye,
ankle high and shining like silk
where the wind
shows in ripples
and momentary lanes
that lead the eye
          to no easy cure.
No one is here.
No hand on my shoulder.
No angel voice from a gold mist.
And the cold
blue air refuses rescue,
tells me again:
You lost it last night.

So the altarboy still in me

goes to the garage,
gets the ladder and hangs
her Christmas gift,
the Duncraft feeder,
and fills it with seed.
He retreats.
Hours pass.
Little improves,
his head still hollow.
Look at him.
The purity of winter
light is a taunt.
Nobody can help
but me
as he watches
at the french doors, waits
for chickadees,
titmice, and a cardinal
I finally allow to arrive.

The sun gets low
above the trees, orange,
and like a fiery poultice
draws the last
of last night's poison.
A shaft of light
ignites that ice in the grass—
a pile of diamonds
still big enough
to buy back the world.

DUST DEVIL

This was New London,
the first station with a rotating sign,
a bright orange SHELL,
and right after I had done six months
in produce at the A & P,
those fast building clouds,
the color of eggplant and endive.
I was gassing a Coupe de Ville
and down Coleman,
which was empty, comes this wind
you could see before hearing—

a twirling column of trash,
a drunk wobbling toward us
with a breathy roar
like the open door of a furnace
before it fell apart
under the big orange SHELL.
"Dust devil," I said, happy to name it.

The customer asked, "What was it?"
"Dust devil," I said again,
savoring the word,
wondering how such a dramatic self-
contained form could die so fast.
"I mean the *total*," he said.
"And catch the windshield, hunh?"
Still staring, I said I would.
"That'll be now, as in today, right?
I gotta make a meeting."

I fumbled coins
and counted change for a fifty,
(a lot of money then)
into his open palm,

as he puffed a cigar
and told me where he was headed,
then said: "Kid, do yourself a favor—
consider some other work."

I watched him disappear,
did myself the favor
of considering
the marvelous trash,
that gathering wind,
and the beautiful SHELL
slowly turning,
against the churning eggplant
clouds about to cut loose.
Even then I knew
impatience was for amateurs,
for people with nothing
better to do than make a meeting
in Bridgeport.

SUBCHASER

Back when we were looking for Russkis
in the skies over our own backyards,
I was also on the lookout for a girl,
nervous too about the blond in the joke,
that blond bombshell easily blown
from here to maternity by a guided muscle.
So I had no steady and tried to stay clear—
at least while my handle was 17 Bravo.
I spent hours after school as a CD spotter,
perched in a firetower outside of town,
an ocean of treetops around me for miles.

"Command Center, this is 17 Bravo," I'd croon,
almost kissing the mike, only after I'd learned
to I.D. at a glance the sharp shapes
of dart-like fighters, Sabres and Starfires,
the squat bombers and lumbering cargoes,
B–52 and C–45, Superfortress and Bugsmasher,
the common MacDonald-Douglass Dakotas,
those Gooney Bird C–47s, and rarer blackbirds,
the Lockheed Neptunes with belly bubble sonar
and long stinger tails. Then the lethal profiles
of MIGs, Ilyushins, Tupolevs I hoped never to see.

But my favorite was the Grumman Subchaser,
the S–2F1 that played cat-and-mouse with our own
subs for practice off the Connecticut coast.
On my first date with Marion, I told her all about
that broad-winged beauty. I told her
you could tell it by sound alone, the lovely
raffling of its twin Wright radials. She listened
with her lips parted and when the last word
fell from mine, came on like a heat-seeker
and down I went in flames,
reappearing on her porch night after night.

Sometimes, in my supercharged Ford, we'd park
off a dirt road by the runway to watch
pilot trainees get the feel of touch and go, going
through preliminaries and intricate maneuvers.
In deep grass by the apron, one June afternoon
before prom, I did a wing-over and lay
on my back, flying upside down, the windsock
stiff, when one of those blackbirds raffled over,
and I whispered my last report: "This is Grumman
S–2F1, wing-tanks full, off on a long reconnaissance,
direction uncertain. Over and out."

ON THE BLUE AGAIN

Because he's on board by himself
        and headed offshore
toward a blind but promising spot,
        he can only duck

under deck for a moment,
        this small dry world, wanting
steerage and constant attention
        on blue hills fallen to gullies.

Through porthole and skylight and
        short teak doorway
he can find a center and frame,
        let's say, a two-second glimpse—

the tall white shaft of Lookout Light,
        a hand-shaped cloud all blue,
the stern and wake fizzing out white
        on green water, dissolving

as terns fling down on minnows.
        And breathing the April air,
bleach and bits of hard-to-get mold
        on this first run,

he might easily be loosed
        from the ache of something lost,
as if it weren't, and, like a child,
        care for nothing

but mastery of all the fleet facets
        of this random moment
when a gull makes a dart of itself,
then labors aloft, its catch flashing.

PAPA

From Bear Island to Cape Lookout,
the choice flats for flounder, the short-cut
channels through salt marsh,
grassy sandspits, and the lone egret, white
as the dazzled sand on Shackleford Banks
where wild horses top the dunes,
manes fired by the sun—
everything unghosted, this map of my own
made close by looking.

So the *Pilar* never came to mind
that morning the ocean dreamed its buoys and sails
until the black diamonds of Lookout Light
disappeared landward
and everything east was unknown,
my first boat
with size enough to reach the Big Blue Water—
"the last wild country," he wrote.

        I had to look harder,
now bound for reefs and the deep wrecks,
I had to memorize
the way flying fish take to the air,
        skittering like crickets before a combine.

I had to study the surface
        as much as my heading
change degrees
of brown, green, to matchless indigo
the closer we got to the Stream,
steering near the yellow rafts of sargasso
where mahi hid and began to hit
our blue and white witches.

The sun searing, gilding the edges
        of shifty blue hills,
I looked and squinted,
catching what maybe he hadn't—
the way shearwaters wavered above the boat,
swung in for the long skim,
and mahi fluoresced at the transom,
turning radiant gold when gaffed into air.

I became my own skipper at last,
boating the black-banded wahoo,
shark-like cobia,

and yellow-fin thick as a football.
Now I could forget that old brown man in a smack
        with his pencil-thick lines,
and young lions sparring on white beaches.

On a breathless noon of blue glass,
more like Papa than I knew, proud of number,
the two hundred pounds already on ice,
        I heard the port-side outrigger pop
and one of the Penn Golds
                    scream out 80-pound test.

Up from the element he thought we had
        instead of religion,
        a great Blue Marlin
in a wild thrash to throw our seawitch and ballyhoo,
tailwalking, then tearing to starboard
so fast the line was frozen straight astern,
a false lead that almost had us miss
his first in a series of ten-foot leaps.

The water exploded
        and this great Blue
        soared straight up
like a sunstruck bar of silver with a bill,

and skied its·six hundred pounds.
No hops and falls,
these were leaps and clean dives
before he suddenly sounded,
gone for two hours,
shame now making its bid
because neither of us
         could tough it alone,
Ed and I taking turns,
sweat-soaked under a burning sky,
that stiff rod between us,
         co-catching—shameful!—
all the while laughing at being beaten silly
by a fish that in the end
we only tagged with red plastic
and released.

         Surely Papa'd spin,
even faster to know
that we were lucky and not exact,
our Great Blue a fluke
caught while after wahoo,
that even with all the backing down of the boat,
our arms ached,
our hands bubbled with blisters.

Yet what stays caught
are those flanks flashing,
the slow back and forth lash of its tail,
sinking back to the clear blue deep—
That and the dreamy sway in the tuna tower
on the way home,
and a last glimpse of that limpid oceanic river
running through the day.

                              for Ed Janosko

63

ANOTHER COUNTRY

On the way to Guayaquil,
    still high in the Andes,
        stalled on a dirt road
    miles from a village,
we were cursing a tire
    for leaving us breathless,
        grease and dirt
    on our hands

when the hazy distance
    advanced a figure
        slowly more precise,
    a dark shape
dumpy as a cupcake
    but thick chested
        with a mountain
    of sticks on his back,
face thrust forward,
    tumpline to forehead.
        In black pants,
    he staggered,
straightening his load
    without stopping.
        Sandals slapping,
    he climbed steadily,
each breath a burst of air,
    the curve taking him
        out of sight, leaving us
    looking at dark spots
of sweat in the dust.

Then higher up,
    that mountain of sticks
        floated left to right

above the tropical florescence
past tilled horizontal rows,
on vertical slopes,
up switchbacks fading
into a region of clouds,
some promise of sleep.

Sometimes when I need him,
that man in sandals
wobbles into sight
through veils of heat,
his breath roaring
like a fire,
wood clacking on his back,
that bronze Incan face,
the load-bearing step
that moves
into a thickening dark.

FLUTEMAN

There's a dirt road that goes deep
      into high desert,
and this time I want to go deeper, further past Price,
into the ancient quiet of Nine Mile Canyon.
It's a lumpy brown sugar trail, sweeter and sweeter
the further it goes
past the remains of a mining town,
ghost rails rusting in sage,
glass chips glinting in the weeds,
      then narrowing
between walls of light siennas
and dark umbers getting higher.

None of our everyday gab and gimme—
only the sandrock glyphs of the Fremonts
who have held their tongues for a thousand years.
The road peters out
so I leave the Jeep, its clever built-in compass,
and trust my feet.
The last safe sound is metal creaking in the heat
quickly lost to the thunder
      of mere footfalls
and the roar of continuous breath
on a steep climb far above the valley floor
in the sweating sun toward
      a ten-foot snake
      and a perfect lizard,
bright orange, peened out of black desert varnish.

Just under foot, darting into a crevice,
the same lizard that served as a model
makes you wonder about the snake
and careful where you place your feet.

Along the ledge are images of ladders,
          hands and faces,
               spirals, spiders, and deer—
mule deer that still graze the wild grasses
far below in the sun
that heats my hatless head
with a crazy feeling
small hunters could be back any second
to reclaim these caves and ledges.
          A head-dressed bow hunter
          or a dark man dipped in varnish,
using a deerbone tool
to peck these totems that blaze out in orange
through a blue-black glaze on the rockface.
          Around the corner,
a child, a woman, and woodsmoke,

but that's the oven sun,
and loss of fluid
so I take the chance
(though there is no path)
of an easier way down through the shade
of cottonwoods hugging the cliff
and come face to face
with a man in a darkened alcove,
a stick figure in a square-topped hat,
arms extended, but crooked for the flute
he must have played right here
in this echo chamber, bent back perhaps
in the ecstasy of a high note.

I sit for a moment to rest and listen.
          A rockchuck yelps.
Then the canyon breathes
as he plays the land
through a deerbone flute,
two, three, four notes
of perfect pitch, the last

held long, then fading
into the breath of the canyon,
a resonant hum drawn out
over rimrock
same color as the sun going down.

VALENTINE

Did I ever tell you that years ago I escaped
the icy sidewalks and falling snow to buy my first

for a girl named Judy? In Kresge's five-and-dime?
Early dark made the front windows into slabs of black,

so with card in hand, I drifted down the aisle
to my favorite spot past the pink lingerie, and dreamed

at a tank teeming with goldfish, watching them
spurt and glide, balance perfectly still, before facing

that brittle outside dark again. Oh, don't worry,
you'll have chocolate, and roses too, but remember

how once, windward of the jetty, we lost the engine?
I drop the anchor quick but those quarry rocks,

blacker for the sun and pale blue water, keep coming
closer and closer. My eyes race down the rope

through thirty feet of water clear as dreamfright
to where the anchor flukes are plowing the bottom,

then catch on coral, halting those ragged black rocks
only ten feet from our hull. Then it was you

who lifted the cowl, found where the coil
wire frayed, and gave us fire again.

So we lingered, engine idling, to watch beneath the boat
a huge school of spade fish shaped and striped

like those french angels our son used to have in his tank.
Suddenly they were gone.

Which is to say, you always take me back
to teenage gold and the primary colors

of coral and communal fish, that pale blue
water on which our down-looking faces float,

slide into each other and eclipse,
as in a dream—one more way

that we merge, rarely guessing how often we drift
into, away from, around, and through.

for Phyllis

BRADFORDS

The house hummed,
a music of small sounds
and unbearable light,
so I pushed myself out.

All the dark day
it was rainy, and stop
after needless stop,
cold in the car,

dim at the drugstore,
the air at Car Care
shattered with shouts,
smoky and blue.

And nothing
at the Roadkill Grill
but the gray gloom
of dug-in drinkers—

a prelude to the clerk
at the cleaners,
who smoked at her face
in the plateglass.

Then the after-rain
dark of the market:
coffee and raisins,
dark bread, red wine,

and Jésus, a bagger,
a kid I've tested
my Spanish on,
glowing through,

chanting
"*Qué pasa, amigo?*"
smiling at nothing
I can see

as I walk outside
into the last of
the first day of spring,
the music of his voice

lighting the Bradfords
all along the esplanade
into full bloom—trees
pruned into bulbs,

a white mist lifting
from an asphalt dark
now different—
an all-day joke on me,

Bradfords the punchline,
making me laugh
then hum my way
back home.

SEQUOIA SEMPERVIRENS

On the south fork of the Eel River
it is hot, oddly deserted, the water
a wonder on my unbooted feet.
I have just hiked back from a grove
where some have been standing
since Christ was a child.

More than thirty feet wide,
close to four hundred high,
three distinct vertical climates.
Only two percent left
of what was here when the Spanish
marched through.

Down river an osprey
teeters in a tight circle above
a pool insisting on the same reflection—
those trees, only two percent,
that church-like nave,
soaring pillars of umber,
sunshafts like flying buttresses
made of gold.

The river whispers to itself.
The osprey swings away on a wider tack
and just as I'm about to plunge,
come up with something flashing,
something appropriate,
essential and deeply true,
an electronic beep disturbs the air.

When I look up, a boy's there
in a Giants cap and jersey—
ghost of an earlier self—
above me on the footbridge

with a cell phone to his ear.
The osprey disappears.
The boy talks to his pal.
"Just waiting for my parents," he says,
"looking at some dumb tree."

ABOVE SPANISH FORKS

This steep trail
we've undertaken together
after stories
that promised us
peregrines at play
in the alpine air.
We cross a wash
full of rubble
from a rockface
we are too close to see.
Now we are easing
along a ledge
that emerges in meadows
above the last stands
of white fir
toward higher regions,
snowfields and limestone
blinded by the sun.

Like airborne otters,
they nip and roll—
360s we're told—
tuck and plunge for fun
or the feel of what they are,
but today they stay away
as if wary of people
looking for something to keep.

The air is thin.
So we sit to need less.
The rocks all around us shine.
A jay insists on itself
like something inside
that won't quite quit,
each squawk opening a silence,

earth-scent, a trickle of snowmelt,
the steady press of the sun.

Now the quiet tunes us
to that unseen plunge and soar,
our faces tilted back,
me looking for her,
she looking for me
with our eyes shut tight.

DISTANCE AT THE DOCKSIDE INN

Diners under blue awnings turn
to watch a two-masted ketch in the channel,
burnished by a low sun. This is the moment
you notice the one person
who hasn't turned, the moment
halyards stop slapping their masts,
her body bent forward, the shoulders bobbing,
her face twisted with tears, the moment
everything is straining to hear
those shouts, cries, and whispers deep inside
a story that is always the same.

The man at the table leans forward,
touching her shoulder, but much too late.
The diners look, then look at their glasses of wine,
the faultless sun, a far-off sail by Monet.
Her torso nods in time
to the waves from a careless runabout.
Across the channel, just above her shoulders,
two wild horses come down the dune
to the shallows, one following the other
along a shelf of hard sand
into a perfect red circle of sun.

SEASCAPE

The moon tricked us out off the reef,
the only boat in the channel that night,
then left us dead in the water, our flare gun
cocked, when mullet start hitting like mad.

Too beautiful, the night sea dreamed us
for contrast, to make us perhaps more precise
about cloud, the wild sculpture it makes,
moon low, yellow on the southern edge.

And color has its own kind of luck.
Last week, I picked up a kid out of gas,
full of manic laughs, two miles off the beach
on a jet ski. "Fuck the sharks," he said.

Who cares if we sort through and mimic
the choice parts of what we hear and see?
Rescued, we'll re-make the seascape,
strewn with moonchips, bright as a mahi.

Nor'easters pick up sand, blast our glass, fog
our ocean view, but mornings still find us eager
for those fishing boats to refine themselves
to simple black shapes adrift on a waste of gold.

EGRET

Nature is a haunted house
—Emily Dickinson

Twilight was losing its color.
On either side of the high-rise bridge,
endless archipelagos of eelgrass spread below me,
far-spaced herons
and egrets like dazzling white flags,
mullet breaking parts of the marsh mirror,
birds in their final moves, feathering off
to a distant tree line of peaks and valleys,
a reminder of vital signs on a screen.

Up close, an egret's white
might be slightly stained
with mud from the thrash of a fish
        and you might be upset
by the greedy gold of its eye
before the beak-stab
and the bull-whip snap of its neck.
        But farther off,
these birds are something else,
that blinding white letter S
made by the same lethal neck
against a wall of tall grass—
it stands for what?
Salvation?   Surrender?

In a depth of field,
still but for the slo-mo stride
or dip of beak,
they might be garden statues,
        placed just so
at inlets or sandspits
in the rich tidal green

to urge inner movement,
                these lone white icons
I saw once in number
at a sunset rookery on Goat Island,
making me think
there must be a law
that has them in heaven at night.
But during the day,
just when we need them,
they touch the eye
                with the right kind of light.

Some days,
just in off the ocean,
under churning black clouds in our boat,
we cross the Beaufort Bar,
and out of the corner of sight,
                that flash of white
is the substance of my mother's prayer
come from a distance beyond belief
to see me·back safe.

As I stood looking down
from the five-story bridge,
an egret,
as if conjured, lifted from reflection,
dipped its long wings into heavy air
and rowed out of sight
to a rookery on the far side
of the bridge.

A sloop passed beneath,
a tear of burnished teak,
with flames at the stern
and two figures trying to douse them.
But that was a trick of distance,
for, a moment later,
as the sloop moved further off,

a scent reached up—
the black and red of grilled meat
that now turned me back
through the dark,
hungry for the colors of home.

FLYING FISH

Halfbeaks, needles, and a dozen more
you'll find only far from shore,
and see them best
when the Gulf Stream
lifts and falls in a glassy trance
        and your eye
is taken by their glittery lift-offs
over water blue as midnight.

A flight longer
than you might have expected
for fins working as wings.
The brief splash
instantly heals and they never rise
again from the same spot.

Like grasshoppers
before blades making hay,
        they flicker off
in singles, coveys, and flocks.
It's not so much the boat
that makes them fly
        in a series of silk rippings
but schools of albacore,
dolphin, and big-eye rising to feed.

Late, docked between piles,
the boat tugging its white lines
at the center of a cat's cradle,
you lie deep in the portside berth.

Skin still radiant,
you breathe resin,
teak oil and sweat, last year's weather
still trapped in the lockers,

your eye in the light of a half moon
wandering over rods
and reels racked along the cabin roof,
the feather lures, bright plugs and drones,

and before long,
        they are flying again
over black mirrored waters,
        skimming flights,
and one, on glowing wings, that lasts and lasts
until an outboard sputters
and first dawn rims the edge.

DAY OF THE WARBLER

I begin to see . . .
when I cease to understand
                    —Thoreau

A leaf-yellow day
and cidery mild in the mountains,

          but eighteen miles offshore
it was clouds down tight as a lid,
and dark when the turnabout wind
came to a boil.

Sizzling swells
had taken our last good words
and left us looking, barely looking
at rodtips, at layers of gray,
at the careless rotation of compass,
gulls gone, not a thing for the eye

          until that bird,
yellow as an autumn leaf,
small as a wren,
          was there,
like a magician's feather flower
sprouting from the tip of my rod.

Boarded by a bird
on the high seas, we were
hijacked to attention,
him blown far from his mates
and resting, us afraid to make
one false move, while he kept us
in his sights
and centered
like a small sun,

finally sparing us
and insisting we see
what to say.

We watched him dart
and hover,
from teak rail to canvas top,
then foot by tiny foot, dark
as an opal
down the Bimini straps
to the windshield,
where he rested,
then switched his stance,
heartbeat high,
keeping to windward,
wings open
to balance the weather,
leaving us
with a lasting yellow,
one small spot
lighting the day.

for Ron Hoag

A GUIDE TO ARRIVAL

All the way to heaven is heaven—
—St. Catherine of Siena

Remove your watch
and pick a place,
the back porch, say.
Expect nothing
when you step out

toward the blue crowns
of hydrangea that draw
attention to the absence
of wind.

Sit on the steps.
Watch the yard
shed its dark colors,
and dogwood tire
of its white meaning.

Don't think
that flicker in the oak
is a May Day
from childhood,
some S.O.S. from the past.
No past at all.

The cat sheds fur
that floats from your hand
like milkweed fluff.

Absorb the stillness,
however momentary,
as if in a photo,

followed by a bird cry
not dying away.

In slow motion steps,
the cat takes
her patchwork fur
and vanishes
into the patchwork shade.
You say her name
but she won't come back.

What else do you want?
Tell yourself nothing
that's not right here,
leaves bursting into light,
light into leaves.

TRAFFICKING WITH VOICES

Tired of talk,
I lowered the headset volume
and instead gave in to the endless mantra
of the single engine Cherokee Arrow.
My friend Ed kept tabs on the instruments,
listened to distant men and women
who moved us from sector to sector
and told him what to do.

I quit looking
at tiny houses, rivers,
and yellow buses full of kids headed home.
Older voices whispered like white sound,
white as the sacred mountains
of the book in my lap.
When I looked up later
from Himalayan peaks on the page,
the towering clouds all around seemed right.

Then specks appeared on the storm scope,
swarms of amber bees due south.
"I know," said Ed. He talked to McGuire Control
while I watched the clouds ahead,
not white any more with azure escapes.
Threads of lightning
stitched them tighter and blacker.

On instruments, you can't climb
until they tell you to, as in Simon Says,
so we waited right into the front
and the sun went out like a bulb.
The book shot from my lap
and hit the cockpit roof. The wings flexed,
and rain crackled like flung gravel.
All dark,

except for the instruments, lightning,
and the whites of Ed's eyes as he worked
to keep control. I thought of the outer
dark from inside its turbulence

and down the aisle, for no reason
I could think of quite,
strode Sister Paulita in the 5th grade,
yanking me from my seat so hard
that my eyeballs rattled
like dice in a black leather cup.
No luck. I was ready for the outer dark
of that freezing New England fire escape
for sneaks, gigglers and cutups
when I heard
the voice of an improbable poem:

Cherokee Triple Seven Zero Delta,
this is McGuire Control,
climb to ten thousand feet
on a heading of one six niner
and stand by for a new vector home.

Later, racing with the moon,
way up in the midnight blue,
me humming that old tune by Vaughn Monroe,
Ed asked what I'd found so funny
down in that storm.
"Remember the nuns," I said,
"how you had to sing alone,
how they'd shake the hell out of you,
how lucky it felt to be heading home after school?"

"We had the brothers," he said,
"now they call it child abuse."
And we laughed like guilty kids again.

Far below our starboard wing,
by itself in a vast space, its nav lights blinking,
a small plane like ours
slowly sank into a bank of clouds that flashed,
every so often, like a broken neon tube.

That lucent voice, almost sourceless, I thought,
and hoped it was talking them through.

ACKNOWLEDGMENTS

Grateful acknowledgement is made to editors of the following publications in which some of these poems or earlier versions of them first appeared:

Aethlon: The Journal of Sport Literature: "Papa";

America: "Catsail";

The Hudson Review: "Owl and Heron";

Calliope: "Gray Removals" and "Beyond French Doors";

Chattahoochee Review: "Not Wasted," "Hunter," and "Sequoia Sempervirens";

Chelsea: "Trafficking with Voices";

Cimarron Review: "Lobsters," "Day of the Warbler," and "Valentine";

Connecticut Review: "Above Spanish Forks";

The Laurel Review: "Ritual on Indian Pier," "After the Perfect Place," and "Dogwood Again";

The Louisville Review: "Bradfords" and "Chalet in Air";

Mind Over Matter: "Ocean Fog";

North Carolina Literary Review: "Egret" and "On the Blue Again";

Poultry: "Leaning Against the Bar at Wrong Way Corrigan's in Greenville, North Carolina";

Poet & Critic: "Big Eddy, Upstream of the Grimesland Bridge";

Poetry: "Woodsmoke" and "Close";

Poetry Miscellany: "Another Country";

Poetry Northwest: "Flying Fish," "Dry Creek," and "Guide to Arrival";

The Sandhills Review: "Dust Devil," "Subchaser," and "Near the Agua Fria";

Seneca Review: "Distance at the Dockside Inn";

The Sewanee Review: "Against Distance" and "Tangier Island";

Southern Poetry Review: "Fluteman" and "After".

"Catsail," "On the Blue Again," "Against Distance," "Lobsters," "Seascape," "Day of the Warbler," "After the Perfect Place," "Ritual on Indian Pier," "Big Eddy, Upstream of the Grimesland Bridge," "Valentine," and "Egret" were first collected and published with other poems as a chapbook entitled *Shorelines* (Greentower Press, 1995).

ABOUT THE AUTHOR

Peter Makuck is Distinguished Professor of Arts and Sciences at East Carolina University where he is also editor of the journal *Tar River Poetry*. He has published five collections of poetry, including *Where We Live* (BOA Editions, 1982) and *The Sunken Lightship* (BOA Editions, 1990); a collection of short stories, *Breaking and Entering*; and a co-edited book of essays on the Welsh poet Leslie Norris. He was the recipient in 1988 of the Brockman Award, given each year for the best collection of poetry by a North Carolinian, and the 1993 Charity Randall Citation from the International Poetry Forum. He lives in Pine Knoll Shores, North Carolina.

BOA EDITIONS, LTD.
AMERICAN POETS CONTINUUM SERIES

Vol. 1   *The Fuhrer Bunker: A Cycle of Poems in Progress*
          W. D. Snodgrass

Vol. 2   *She*
          M. L. Rosenthal

Vol. 3   *Living With Distance*
          Ralph J. Mills, Jr.

Vol. 4   *Not Just Any Death*
          Michael Waters

Vol. 5   *That Was Then: New and Selected Poems*
          Isabella Gardner

Vol. 6   *Things That Happen Where There Aren't Any People*
          William Stafford

Vol. 7   *The Bridge of Change: Poems 1974–1980*
          John Logan

Vol. 8   *Signatures*
          Joseph Stroud

Vol. 9   *People Live Here: Selected Poems 1949–1983*
          Louis Simpson

Vol. 10   *Yin*
          Carolyn Kizer

Vol. 11   *Duhamel: Ideas of Order in Little Canada*
          Bill Tremblay

Vol. 12   *Seeing It Was So*
          Anthony Piccione

Vol. 13   *Hyam Plutzik: The Collected Poems*

Vol. 14   *Good Woman: Poems and a Memoir 1969–1980*
          Lucille Clifton

Vol. 15   *Next: New Poems*
          Lucille Clifton

Vol. 16   *Roxa: Voices of the Culver Family*
          William B. Patrick

Vol. 17   *John Logan: The Collected Poems*

Vol. 18   *Isabella Gardner: The Collected Poems*

Vol. 19   *The Sunken Lightship*
          Peter Makuck

Vol. 20   *The City in Which I Love You*
          Li-Young Lee

Vol. 21   *Quilting: Poems 1987–1990*
          Lucille Clifton

Vol. 22   *John Logan: The Collected Fiction*

Vol. 23   *Shenandoah and Other Verse Plays*
          Delmore Schwartz

Vol. 24   *Nobody Lives on Arthur Godfrey Boulevard*
          Gerald Costanzo

Vol. 25   *The Book of Names: New and Selected Poems*
          Barton Sutter

Vol. 26   *Each in His Season*
          W. D. Snodgrass

Vol. 27   *Wordworks: Poems Selected and New*
          Richard Kostelanetz

Vol. 28   *What We Carry*
          Dorianne Laux

Vol. 29   *Red Suitcase*
          Naomi Shihab Nye

Vol. 30   *Song*
          Brigit Pegeen Kelly

Vol. 31   *The Fuehrer Bunker: The Complete Cycle*
          W. D. Snodgrass

Vol. 32   *For the Kingdom*
          Anthony Piccione

Vol. 33   *The Quicken Tree*
          Bill Knott

Vol. 34   *These Upraised Hands*
          William B. Patrick

Vol. 35   *Crazy Horse in Stillness*
          William Heyen

Vol. 36 *Quick, Now, Always*
         Mark Irwin

Vol. 37 *I Have Tasted the Apple*
         Mary Crow

Vol. 38 *The Terrible Stories*
         Lucille Clifton

Vol. 39 *The Heat of Arrivals*
         Ray Gonzalez

Vol. 40 *Jimmy & Rita*
         Kim Addonizio

Vol. 41 *Green Ash, Red Maple, Black Gum*
         Michael Waters

Vol. 42 *Against Distance*
         Peter Makuck

12

12

POETRY

"The poetry of Peter Makuck does for the coastal waters of North
Carolina what Wallace Stevens did for the Florida Keys, and Robinson
Jeffers for Big Sur. He revives in language the very look, feel, and
smell of beach and wetlands, and gives a human measure to the
complex imbrication of shore, sky and sea."

— Emily Grosholz

"Peter Makuck's poems are as beautiful and well-made as the best
poems of his contemporaries. What sets them apart from and above
virtually all of them, however, is their *ethos*, their attentiveness to the
world outside the self and their capacity to love: people, creatures,
landscape. Makuck's poetry shows us not only how to see, but
how to live."

— Jonathan Holden

BOA
EDITIONS
LIMITED

260 East Avenue
Rochester, NY 14604

$12.50

Design: Geri McCormick
Cover Photo by Ray Scharf

ISBN 1-880238-45-4

90000>

EAN

8869 5183 30

01/02/98   MAB